Depression

Who's Afraid of the Big, Bad Wolf?

By

John Lipscombe

My thanks go especially to my wife who's spent so much time putting up with me and supporting me, even though it must be almost impossible for her to understand what I have been through. I love her for the unconditional love she continues to show me.

I'd also like to thank Harriet who's positive spark could light a thousand candles and the professionals who have helped to guide me through my depression in a most generous and caring way.

Depression – Who's afraid of the big bad Wolf?

Content

Introduction

The + and - effect

This is probably the biggest thing I will tell you about in my book and if it's the only thing you take away you'll have made my day! The plus and minus effect is something I've thought about continually through my life and you may have done so too. You can make a lot of decisions based around it. For instance, if you look at the various things in your life, do they score a plus, or a minus? There are so many sayings that support this. Is your glass half full, or half empty? There are always two paths you can take, is it hot or cold, light or dark, happy or sad, rewarding, unrewarding? What are the pros and cons? For every action you take there will be a positive or a negative consequence. It's not rocket science, but it is a great tool for establishing the direction you need to take in life and a simple way to manage things.
Through every chapter put yourself in that scenario and figure out what it is that make things a plus or a minus. You'll recognise them straight away and it will help you to make the right decision.

Ok, so here's the thing, I'm not a doctor, I don't have a PHD in psychology, or any training in dealing with mental health problems, however, I have suffered with severe depression and have spent a lot of time trying to deal with it by firstly, understanding it, secondly coming to terms with it and thirdly working with it on a day to day basis. I'm nobody special, I don't have all the answers, I still suffer with depression now and then, I just happen to have gained some experience in how to go through the process and come out safely on the other side.

Interestingly, it's something like one in four people in the UK who will experience some sort of mental health problem, but women are more likely to seek treatment. What that says to me is that there are a huge amount of people, men and women, who are saying "depression....what me?" It's not a visible rash, a broken arm, you don't see people hobbling around because they're suffering with depression and so sadly a lot of the time depression isn't even considered to be a medical illness. Thankfully that is changing now and the government and health services are doing much more to recognise and treat the condition as a serious illness. Sadly, like any other serious illness, people can die from it!

So how do you know if you're just having a bad day, or if you're actually suffering from anxiety, or depression? Read through this book and keep asking the question, "is this me?" deep down you probably already know the answer. More than just reading my book though, it's really important that you talk to people, get advice from every professional on offer, from your GP to counselling. Seek professional help from the start and use my book to compliment your treatment.

I've kept the book short, let's face it the last thing you need right now is to be wading through pages of a book that would give War and Peace and run for its money. It's a book you can dip in and out of though. I'm sure you'll mark out the chapters of the book that are useful to you. I know people who say you should keep your books in good condition. I say fold down the pages, scribble on them. Make notes. It's your book, make it yours and you'll get the best value from it.

I'm also throwing in sections that I call 'A Slice of Life'. It's situations in daily life that can be very frustrating as well as funny if you allow them to be. It's the world trying to get a piece of you and you need to personally figure out what these issues are and how to deal with them. They're just a few of my own personal choices plucked from the tree of despair! You'll probably recognize them and that's the trick. If you see these situations coming, you can do several things, avoid them, laugh at them, or confront them on a daily basis and say "No". The annoyances of the day, and there can be many, won't go away. You can't change the world, but you can change the way you feel about it. Never collect these confrontations, you're just trying to re affirm your belief that we live in a crap world! Laugh at them, understand them. Let them go.

Even if you come to the conclusion that you're not suffering from depression, hopefully some of my suggestions will help you to lead a more stress free life and at the very least understand when you're having a bad day. On the other hand if you are depressed, you will probably start pointing your finger at the pages saying wildly "that's me". In that case hopefully we can go on a journey together and find a better way, for you and all the people you love.

The problem with depression is that you think nobody really cares about you, but that will almost always turn out to be wrong and not the opinion of the people around you. It's more likely that they just don't know you've got it. Like I said before depression doesn't come up like a rash, there's no bandage wrapped around your head, it's not a massive banner you wave everywhere you go.

"Morning John, you're hobbling a bit this morning."

"Yes, a touch of the depressions playing me up today!"

Many people with depression have it because they spend their lives trying to please everybody, all of the time. YOU CAN'T ALWAYS BE THE LIFE AND SOUL OF THE PARTY. Accept this fact and accept that you're only human. Most of us actually cover it up pretty well. (That's what we do). When I told my wife I'd been diagnosed with depression she said that the only give away, if there was any, was that I'd stopped whistling. (So I must have been annoying before because apparently I do that a lot!)

SUMMARY
Look at the plus and minus effect.
Seek help from the professionals.
Make your own scribbles and notes in the book.
Ask the question... Is this me?

<u>Signposts</u>

Understanding who you are now and how you got to this place will help put you in the driving seat when it comes to breaking down the problems into manageable, coherent chunks. It's a bit like knowing who your ancestors were, suddenly it clicks as to who you are today. If you look back at your life can you see times that might have shown that you were susceptible to falling into a depressive state? It may have started last year, or twenty years ago, but go back as far as you can and start logging events in your mind. Write them down if it helps. (I've left blank pages at the back)

Let me show you what I dug up about myself............

When I was five or six I remember having a deep conversation with my father. (Unusual at that age). I wanted answers to questions that my dad didn't have. Why did I feel sad? Why did I sometimes find the world I lived in such a terrible place? What was my purpose for just being? At a young age it's clear that I was already leaning towards a negative disposition.

At the age of ten I remember hanging my head out of an upstairs window and just looking down at the ground below. If I jumped what would happen? Would I be sorry for doing it? Would I be transported to a better place? Would anyone care? Of course they would, but at that tender age I couldn't be sure. I did also wonder what we might be having for tea that night too! I was extremely confused.

Through my teenage years I struggled to fit in, finding everything that all my peers were up to pointless. I was looking for a guiding light, some eureka moment to show me the way...there wasn't one. I muddled along and don't get me wrong, I had a great childhood, secure in a loving family. I couldn't have asked for a better upbringing. My father was always the joker, he could really make us laugh. My mother was the warmth and loving protection that every child seeks. And my brother and sisters were great mates to hang around and play with, we hardly ever argued, unusual eh! It wasn't them, it was me.

I left school with not too many qualifications and yet I'm not stupid, honest! However, there are no obtainable qualifications for being the school clown and that's pretty much how I got through those years. I wanted to be liked. I wanted my class mates to laugh. It also stopped me getting beaten up and I managed to sidestep the odd wedgie! For three or four years I managed retail shops in London, but instead of flourishing I found that I was happier, if that's the right word, in my own company. I can't begin to count the excuses I made up for not meeting up with friends, or having a night out. It's only now when looking back on those early years I can see, I was suffering from anxiety and depression. I couldn't tell anyone about it ....because I didn't know I had it.

In my twenties life was great. I obtained contracts abroad working as a piano player. Somebody paid me to go off and see the world. I had no responsibility, no bills to pay. I didn't even have to worry about what I was going to eat from day to day, it was all their handed to me on a plate, so to speak.

Eventually my wife and I decided to unpack the suitcases. And returning to the UK with no jobs and no prospects, we started a family. Having our daughter was the most wonderful and meaningful thing that I've ever done with my life. Reminding yourself of things like that when you're depressed can be great therapy. However, anyone who's brought up a family will know how hard that can be. The lack of sleep will cloud your judgement for a start. That's something that you should think seriously about. Discipline yourself when it comes to how much sleep you get. Try and stick to a strict pattern. Figure out just how much sleep you need per night. When you're not tired your thought processes become a lot sharper, positive not negative. At the very least recognize that it might be sleep deprivation that's clouding your ability to make clear decisions. I know it may be hard to do in the first place. There were times when I would stay up until three, or four in the morning just trying to gather my thoughts. You can't! I have the added problem of suffering with sleep apnoea. I forget to breathe which causes me to constantly wake. In the morning I feel like I need to go straight back to bed. The lack of oxygen means my body hasn't had that lovely peaceful time to mull over which bits of the anatomy it should repair first. So is it any wonder I felt fed up and grouchy all day when trying to function in a dream state. I'm pleased to say that through medical help I now have that under control.

A funny moment happened to me at work one day when I was suffering really badly. I work in a small studio at a radio station with no window, no daylight and there I cut audio amongst other things. The boss came in one day and asked if I was ok? Yes, fine, I told him. He laughed and explained that ten minutes earlier he had come in to my studio to find me asleep, sitting bolt upright facing my computer screen with my hand still holding the mouse! When he was sure I hadn't suddenly died he had left me to carry on oblivious to the rest of the world. (How very understanding!)
I could also manage to fall asleep whilst in mid conversation with my wife, but it's probably fair to say that with every situation there are winners and losers.

The busy life of bringing up a family means you have less time to consider your own wellbeing and so you take a step back from *you*. This applies to both parents. Even if the child care and work load are evenly spread, that won't stop you being exhausted. It's as if this new, tiny little being is daring you to fail! In some respects it's obviously right to step back from '*you*', but it means that we do stop asking the questions, "Where am I going?" and "what's my importance in life?"

And so we come to the part of my life where depression reared its ugly head in all its glory. I'd spent years being with my daughter, playing with her, doing activities as a family, trying to be the best I could be.....and then she grew up. And so one Christmas I found myself putting up the decorations by myself, making mince pies and cranberry sauce, by myself.

Without warning, although I should have seen it coming, that side of my life just stopped. It was as if someone had flipped a switch. I was already depressed, but this situation brought it home to me. Of course your children will leave, of course your life is ever changing, but I realised I couldn't cope with any sudden change.

This was all coupled with other compounding factors. I live in the north of England, it can rain a lot, (you know it's summer when the rain gets warmer!), it's really dark in winter, it's cold and I'd ended up in a job working in a radio station studio with no day light. And that's when it all went wrong. I was lucky enough to be still mentally aware that something drastic was wrong and made the decision that I would do something about it, knowing I couldn't remain in this twilight world. I was also very fortunate to have a wife, who although had no understanding of what my depression was like, why should she, could support me and be there when I needed her. It's one of the things I'll talk about later on, but if you don't already have someone close to you that you can talk to, try and find someone. Even if it's just a work colleague, or a long lost aunt, sound them out. You will find that the hardest thing is telling someone how you're feeling. It's amazing how quickly people will come on board and try to support you though.

So you can see from my life experiences that the signs were all there, I'd just over looked them. It's not surprising that we come stumbling and crashing into depression, we don't spend enough time surveying ourselves.

It may not be just about the person you have become, or the situations you have found yourself in over the years...... its modern day life too. Don't blame it all on yourself. You're a product of the ever changing world we live in. With every step forward in modern development I believe our lives can sometimes take a considerable step backwards. I'll take you through that a bit further on in the book.

SUMMARY
Take a look at your life, what were the signs, when did it really take hold and why?
Are you struggling with sleep issues?
Find someone you can talk to.

A Slice of Life

Physically, mentally and financially the world seems to be clambering at your door to get another little slice of you. Here's something that for me sums up the frustrating, clamouring, greedy world we live in. Top selling! Imagine you have a few pounds in your pocket, enough for a coffee. You go and buy your coffee and at the point of sale you're asked, "is that everything today?" The suggestion is that you haven't really thought about it. Yes you have, you wanted a coffee didn't you? "Any pastries to go with that today?" No, you still just want the coffee whether it's today, tomorrow, or the next day. Today you just want a coffee! You hand over your money and then..... "would you like a bottle of water for just a pound today?" JUST A COFFEE, PLEASE!!!!!!

And it happens when you go and buy something as mundane as a battery. "Would you like any stamps today?" No, you're not posting the batteries anywhere, you're just going to take them home in your pocket and STICK THEM IN A TORCH! "Would you like any of these chocolate bars for a pound today?" Do you know what, you only came in to buy a newspaper, but you can bet your life you'll get home and at page five, your vision will cloud over and you'll realise, you can't read a paper without shoving a couple of squares of cheap chocolate IN YOUR MOUTH!!

Top selling is here to stay so get used to it. Laugh about it now and then, it's just the

world trying to be clever. Just a note though....
don't laugh at the salesperson, they're just
doing what they're told to........ and they may be
suffering from a cheeky bout of depression too!

I only wanted a coffee

I only wanted a coffee, black, to take away
But would I like a cake, some stamps, anything else to buy today?
No just an Americano, I'm *so* not having a moan
But I don't need chocolate for a quid, or a top up for my phone!
It's a world where all is sell, sell, sell, and it really is ok
But I'm just going to take the coffee THAT I WANTED TO BUY TODAY!
I'm going to toughen up and no one will draw me in
They'll not sell me some useless crap that'll end up in the bin
The sales brigade are here for good, they'll never go away
But I only want a coffee
....black, to take away!

<u>Can you visualise your depression?</u>

So now we've signposted the fact that this was always probably going to happen to you, based on your previous life experiences and the demands of the world around you today. You've actually taken the first steps to dealing with it, just by understanding how it happened.

Visualising how your depression feels is a really useful tool when you get further down the road. If you can see it as a tangible thing, you'll be able to differentiate between bouts of depression and the times when you're just having a bad day. Let's face it, we all have bad days, but we get over it and start a fresh the next morning. If you're depressed you need to know the best way you can put into place all the measures that will help you control it.

I visualised my depression as a big, black heavy blanket. It took me a while to come up with this, but eventually the visual aid matched my emotions completely. The blanket had been thrown over me and try as I might, I could not get out, I could not regain entry into the real world. It made me feel as if someone had said that I should stay there under the blanket and that was that. I came up with this because I have a fear of small spaces and being unable to breath. It's all because as a child I would turn myself around in my bed and wake up with my head at the bottom, trapped in the blankets that were tightly tucked into the mattress. This may, or may not be you, but my depression constantly threw up the positive and negative, in the form of light and dark, good and bad, worth and worthlessness, even heavy and light. Ask yourself these questions, if you could weigh more, or less....which would you choose? If you could live in darkness, or sunlight...which would you choose? Is it better to love or hate? If you could be of good or bad character...which would you choose? So the blanket was dark not light, heavy not weightless. And with all its suppression I began to think of it as my gaoler's gown.

Visualising your state of mind can help as it gives you something to recognise, confront, deal with and even talk to. My local GP calls it 'talking to the elephant in the room'. This has been key to any kind of success I've had, as it allows me to be one step ahead of the peaks and troughs, to manage them before they manage me. It's also a great tool when people close to you ask, "what does it feel like to be depressed?" It may not give them a complete answer, but it's your stock answer and will give them something to take away, helping them to be a part of the process, nurturing the support you need from them. So whether it's a heavy blanket, a sense of being pulled under water, being stifled, unable to breath, the elephant in the room, whatever you visualise, make it work and visualise it whenever a wave of anxiety, or depression comes to call.

You will feel more empowered if you can master this, like knowing who's outside knocking on your door before you open it. Let's face it we all like to feel as though we have the upper hand now and then. One note of warning though, there may come a point when you take a step backwards. That depression will sneak up on you, and not wishing to be too crude, will bite you in the arse! The learning process for anything in life can be like this. You think you've mastered the skill of driving a car and then, just for a second, you lose your concentration and bang, you clip the curb.

One final thing to note about visualisation is this. It will look like something suppressive, or debilitating, because of the nature of your emotions, but don't let it become a monster that will haunt you. It's not something you should be scared of. In the end that heavy blanket will be like an old friend that you outwitted and saw coming. No more than a wily old fox....... or a big bad wolf!

SUMMARY
Visualise your depression.
Don't let it become a monster.
Be ready to succeed AND fail, it's just the beginning.

A Slice of Life

When people say things like "folk don't know how lucky they are. In my day we didn't have all this technology to help". That's very true, but I'm a firm believer that all this technology that we have today only compounds the problems in our lives. We're expected to make all our transactions on line, even when websites might not be very clear, your broadband is slow and your computer is liable to crash at any moment. You can get something delivered, but nobody gives you a proper time of day. Between 0800 and 1300, 1300 and 1800! What kind of a service is that? And when the said product arrives, you have to build it yourself. Didn't people in factories do that once upon a time? And then there's, "in my day we just used good old pen and paper". Great, but we have to use texts, emails, facebook, twitter, etc and it's relentless. And because we are so accessible at all hours of the day we never switch off. How many times have you spent your evening sorting out work related issues via text and email and if you're self-employed you probably never stop working at all. Technology was supposed to make our lives easier, (if you believe the old days of Tomorrow's World.) Well that didn't happen! Improvements in technology just meant that one person could take on more aspects of a job. One nil to the employers. So, now that one person can do more work, the rest get made redundant. Two nil to the employers and guess what, we just found another reason for depression to come knocking at your door.

Work! You're either working like a crazy person at your job, or sitting at home thinking "How come they made me redundant?" None of it is a personal vendetta against you, it's just the world we live in.

Upon these hills

As I wandered across these vast open fells
It gave me comfort to my spirit
For my mind has lain in vacuous hells
And I am forced to live it
For when the blanket of despair is thrown
across my human wealth
I can no more cry out in protest, than whimper
at my sorry self
It allows me nothing of my day, but saps the
goodness as I stay
Beneath the blanket of despair, I cannot fight,
no strength to spare
I walk and talk and yet brought down
By this heavy cloth, this gaolers gown
And so upon these fells so vast, I shed my
sadness, demons cast
For in this place my head is still, I find my
meaning on a hill

Achievements

Without even analysing your symptoms of depression you can deal with some of your issues and begin your road to recovery with self-affirming strategies. This comes back to the positive and negative side of things. Your job is to create a positive sense of wellbeing around you and you do it in very small ways to begin with.

The chances are you've stopped doing all the things you used to love doing because you just can't find it in you to be bothered, or you're too busy pleasing everyone else. In a state of depression everything feels pointless, but you know that already. It isn't, but just telling yourself that won't make a difference. It's time, in some small way, to stop your mind ruling your life. You need to format your mind by formatting your week. It's no good saying, "I'll start riding my bike again." When will you start riding your bike again? Timetable your week. If you have one small window of opportunity on a Monday afternoon, book it in. It may be something you haven't done for years, or something you've always wanted to do. I decided to take up the saxophone. My wife will tell you how amazed she was at my playing. Who knew I could make a wind instrument sound like a very poorly donkey! She right, but it doesn't matter. If you want to paint an oil painting and they all turn out rubbish, it doesn't matter. You don't have to be the next Turner. Enjoy the textures, the smells, the radio on in the background, the brew half way through creating your masterpiece. This isn't about success, it's about 'doing', it's about you for your sake, not others.

Planning is everything and it's probably not what you feel like doing, but start small, just one activity a week. Get used to doing something for you and you alone. After a while you can start adding more activities to your week. What you're trying to achieve is a healthy balance to your life between work, home life and your life. To put it bluntly, there's a lot of crap in our lives that we have to deal with and there's no getting away from that, but how much easier it would be to put up with it all if we off set it with something enjoyable to do in our lives. Once again it's the plus and minus, the light and dark. Start filling your life with light and the dark stuff won't seem so bad.

Here's another plus and negative in the shape of 'big' and 'small' scenario. My wife and I were working on a cruise ship many years ago. To cut a long story short, the cruise director was giving us a hard time, trying to make us do work that was way outside our contract. We refused and he threatened to throw us off the ship. The situation was resolved eventually, but in the heat of the ongoing situation there was something we did.

The ship anchored off the tiny Greek island of Patmos. We took the tender ashore and from there took a walk up the hill and away from the little port. Before long we were really high up and looking down across the sea. The ship looked tiny and it reminded us that this was a tiny aspect of our lives, it was a tiny speck. It was nothing in the grand scheme of things.

So remember, things don't always go as you'd like, but weigh up the negatives. How big a deal are these things in your life? Also, the more you balance your life with pleasurable things, (without turning it into a world of Hedonism), the less focus you will put on your problems. You can polarise your problems if you're not careful. Accept they exist of course, but put them slightly out of reach.

Fitness and food should also be part of your achievement programme. It's a known fact that we comfort eat and lack the will to exercise when we're depressed and yet, the two things that can really help minimise depression are a proper diet and good exercise.

SUMMARY
Find an activity to do.
Plan an activity in to your week.
Success is enjoyment not the finished article.
How's your diet?
Exercise?

A Slice of Life

For me, the daily confrontation of advertising, just feeds the relentless wave of stress and strain brought to our doors. We need to be strong and say "no" in a firm but polite manner. Take control. If you want to buy something make sure it's your decision! I bought a fridge for £150, yes, bottom end of the range. At the point of sale I was asked, would I like to insure my product for the first twenty four months? This would cover all repairs, but not the light bulb! Now I'm thinking, do they have any pride in the product they're selling? Firstly it shouldn't go wrong, IT'S NEW!!! Secondly, it seems to me that nobody expects anything to last beyond two years anymore. Anyway, the devil's advocate in me starts asking the question, "can you insure the light bulb as well?" The sales assistant looks at me like I'm crazy, I'm not, though I am suffering with depression! Apparently I could quite easily 'tamper' with the light bulb and render it faulty then it wouldn't be a genuine fault. And he must be right because every time I go into the fridge and reach for the cheddar a part of me just wants to give that bulb a good old wrap with my knuckles, just to see if I can indeed render it BUSTED! That way I could jump into my car drive back up the motorway, wasting petrol and an hour of my day and wave said item in smug assistants face!

Anyway, if the product you buy goes wrong within a reasonable time (a year or two depending on the product and it's use), the shop is obliged to make good on the product, with a replacement, or a repair. So, to all the retailers, cold callers, sales teams and anyone else who thinks they can make a living out of making you enter into a contract that you don't need, or can't afford, you say "NO!!"

Gratitude

It's very common in a state of depression to forget all the great things we have in our lives. We're not in the right place to consider them, there's too much else crowding in on us mentally. However, this is something that should be planned into the day. Here's a tip on keeping things really easy to remember without having to write everything on a weekly planner. Decide on something that you see all the time, or something you carry around. For example, every time you go through your front door, start thinking about all the great things you have in your life. How about finding a small object that means something to you? Keep it in your pocket and every time you touch it, start thinking about what you're grateful for. I've even done it by placing a brightly coloured sticker just to the side of my computer at work and every time I looked at it I started running through the list of all the things I was grateful for. You have to find a mechanism to make you do this otherwise you won't get into the habit.

So what difference does this make to our recovery? Well, for a start it's reminding you of all the good things around you, be it people, animals, your work, or just the great TV you bought to watch all your favourite shows on. Straight away it smacks of achievement. What do you know, you're not so useless after all, it's not so bad and there's some good stuff going on! Drinking in a little positivity can seriously quench your emotional thirst buds.

The second thing being grateful does for you is to get your mind used to having positive thoughts again. You'd got to a point where it just didn't do that anymore. That small rock in your pocket, that sticker on your computer is the catalyst that drives you to a more positive state many times a day without you having to consciously think to do it. Imagine if you just decided to think about being grateful every hour. Sometimes you'd hit it bang on, other times you'd be engrossed in what you were doing, or distracted by others and guess what, it stops getting done. It's a bit like promising yourself that you're going to lose weight in the New Year. How many of us say that and then fail. You need to have a plan to make it work.

Now you have to decide what it is you're going to be grateful for. Try and make it a wide variety, not too long a list, but things that are really important to you. Here's an idea of headings that you could go for....family members, pay day, the countryside, the car, technology (ipad, laptop, etc...), your house, your health (we know your mind's not in great shape, but can you walk, talk, swing your arms about? Whatever part of your health remains, that's what you're grateful for). I typed my list onto a small piece of paper and kept that in my pocket, it just made it easier to kick-start my brain. If you're using a list make sure you don't recite it, make every line meaningful.

So, who are you going to tell your grateful? Well you could just shout it into the thin air, but as human beings we are much more used to communicating face to face, even if that is visually in our minds. There's far much more power in having somebody to tell stuff too. It will also make you feel more passionate about what you're saying, what you believe. If you're religious you've got the upper hand. You will naturally talk to God. However, if you're not religious that doesn't mean that you can't talk to someone and be grateful.

I was brought up as a Catholic, changed to the Church of England and then erred on the side of agnostic in my late twenties with the opinion that just about every war in the worlds was sectarian. I know that's not strictly true in this modern day world. There are some very bad people in the world who will use religion as an excuse for committing terrible war crimes and some wonderful groups in society who use their faith to bring about peace in our world. If I was going to pray it would be to ask that these people and their faith in God and humanity would one day bring the world to a more peaceful place. It's also worth remembering that we live in a much more stable place than centuries ago, but with the advent of news reporting it can still feel as if the world is going downhill in a hand cart!

So, if you have a strong religious faith, that will probably help you, but you may have always been an atheist. Whatever your thoughts and beliefs it's time to find someone to be grateful to. This is how I worked it out.

All the things around me that I'm grateful for came from somewhere. They are here by the very nature that we are also here, on this planet. We are on this planet because of the first living organism that started off the whole chain reaction of creating life. So I decided that, for me, nature would be the thing I was grateful to. Then, as I did with depression, I made it visual. I decided that although I was talking to nature, it would be a very grand, powerful, perfect and beautiful nature. So when I was being grateful I would tell it to the Goddess of Nature. This is not about starting some new weird religious cult, far from it. The reason for creating this image is because I didn't have religion in my life. I'd like to think that when I die, if it turns out there is a heaven, I'll be judged on how I've lived my life and not on which team I supported......unless it's Chelsea!

Phew! I think I managed to get around the whole sensitive issue of religion without excluding anyone! Just to add to this, religious faith (though I don't have any) is a wonderful and powerful thing. I was standing in the car park where I work and the Salvation Army have premises next door. I could hear the brass band playing and everyone singing, 'love Changes Everything'. It was so emotionally charged that I couldn't help thinking they were right. Love can truly change everything.

So spend some time thinking about the person you are going to use to be grateful to. If you get stuck for someone by all means use the Goddess of Nature. She's a lovely person when you get to know her and has a few places left on her books too!

<u>SUMMARY</u>
What are you grateful for?
Make a list.
Find a mechanism that helps you go through
this mental process.
Who are you talking to?
Who is *your* God?

A Slice of Life

Another financial catch these days involves your teeth. Once upon a time you just went along to your local NHS dentist and they had a poke around with a metal pointy object. At that point you were told your teeth were in great shape, or you need some work doing. A quick gargle with the pink liquid and you were out of there. Not anymore. It's more and more difficult to find an NHS dentist these days as they've all gone private. What does this mean? I'll tell you what it means. Firstly they'll take £20 - £30 off you every month 'just in case' you need any work doing. However, you can bet your life when the work needs doing, it won't cover your particular treatment. There is the option of paying nothing monthly and then getting slammed with a massive bill.

So, how about I take £30 of my money every month and save it somewhere. Every year I've got £360 and if I need any work doing it will go towards the cost, whatever the treatment.

Let's also remember, these private dentists are a business, they're there to make money! The last time I went to a private dentist was two and a half years ago. Here's what they actually said. "Well Mr Lipscombe everything is looking great, you obviously floss regularly." I smiled up at the lady. I think she smiled back, but I couldn't tell with the face mask and all. And if she did smile it was because she was doing a few calculations in her head. "That filling at the back will need replacing soon though, you better make another appointment with the receptionist. And perhaps, if you've got time today you could stop by the hygienist's room down the corridor?"

All of a sudden the man with great teeth is getting slammed for £60 for the hygienist, £40 for the check-up and £300 for a filling that I may, or may not need. I know we need to take care of our teeth, but two and a half years later and my filling is still good! As with the sales assistant, you should never get angry with these people, they're just doing their job and trying to make a living. After all, they will have spent years at dental school so why shouldn't they make a living. If you want a great service then that's where you should go. I'm just using them as an example, but what I'm saying is, make sure you're aware of all the facts and only enter into something if it's definitely the right thing for you.

Small steps to change

So far we've talked about do you have depression, when did it start, how to recognise it and what to be grateful for in a relentless world that we're calling 'a slice of life' and achievements. So let's talk about how to make the things you want to achieve work.

Being grateful for all the things around you is a really good start to positive mental state, but now you need to look at what you can actually do to make your life a more interesting and positive one. Let's face it you've spent all this time telling yourself that life is worthless, pointless and that you yourself are also worthless, that everything you do counts for nothing. IT'S NOT TRUE! For whatever reason, you've been given the chance to walk upon this earth and that fact shouldn't be taken lightly. It's true that there are some questions about life that are just too big to ask, or find an answer to. Why are we here? When will it end? What happens after that? You've got enough to think about so stop asking "why am I here?" and start asking "what can I do whilst I'm here?" You have as much reason and purpose to make a different to yourself and those around you as anyone else.

What you do with your life now can be as wide ranging as taking half an hour to be by yourself, with your own thoughts, whilst eating a cheese sandwich, to giving back to society and end up as managing director of a worldwide charitable organisation. From now on it's about bringing value to your life, to be able to see the value of what you have done with each day. You may look back at the day you've just had and ponder how run of the mill it has been, but search that day and you will find something that brought value to you, or the people around you.

I'm guessing that 95% of your time, or even more, is being spent doing things that you have to do. We all have to take the bins out, wash the dishes, take the kids to school, but have you built so many of these things into your life that you've stopped thinking about all the other 'doing' stuff? Again, it's about looking back through your life. Take a peek at how it looked before it was filled with complications and demands. What did you just do because you wanted to? Did you sit in a darkened room listening to music? Did you sew? Did you beaver away in your garage making things out of wood? Were you a singer in a band, a bit of a thespian, a poet, a painter? Did you love cooking? What was it you did for no other reason than the fact that you just enjoyed doing it? Churchill spent his time trying to save the world and in his spare time was building a wall in his garden. I'm pretty sure he could have paid someone to do that, but it was his project for no other reason than it brought him great satisfaction.

This is where you need to start, but don't go over the top! Start small and decide on one thing that you're going to do. It may be a re awakening of something from your past, or a new project, that one thing you've always wanted to do. Set some goals, but start with just one project.

So you've decided to take up painting again, you loved art lessons at school, continued for a while after that, then stopped when life got in the way. Here's a good moment to start filling in a page at the back of the book! Start by looking at your week and where there might be a window of opportunity. Perhaps on Monday you get home slightly earlier from work and make a meal............MAKE A GREAT SANDWICH INSTEAD! Even if it's just an hour doing something you love, set it in stone and don't allow anything to stop you. Make it a really important event, everything else can wait. Monday at six is painting time so be ready to do that. Here's a small tip, if your new project is going out to sing in a choir that's fine, but if it's anything at home that requires setting up, try and create a space to do that in. Sometimes we can't be bothered to do things if it means getting lots of equipment out, or clearing the dining room table. It's great if you've got a spare room to go to, but if you haven't it might be a case of setting up in a corner of a room and putting headphones on whilst someone else watches the TV.

Whatever you have to do to make sure you're set up to start your project in the allotted time, do it. Also, making this part of your living space reminds you that you have something in your life that isn't a 'job', or a 'chore', it's you taking control of your life.

So now you've started a project do not get hung up with, "it's not very good, I'm rubbish at this." As we said earlier, this isn't about making a well-crafted cabinet, painting a masterpiece, or becoming the next world famous singing superstar, it's about how it makes you feel. For that one hour are you happy? Have you managed to forget about all the stresses and strain in your life? For one hour a week you could be adding happy juice to your glass of positive mental state.

It could take weeks, or months to get this right, to get to the point where the people around you regard it as normal, "oh it's your painting hour!" let's be honest though, sometimes you have to actually be pro-active to make things happen. Things don't just happen, or just come your way in life. You have to seek them out, actively chase your dreams. It's the same with this simple act once a week, you have to make it happen.

In time you may find that you're grabbing back another sneaky hour of your life to do a bit more 'you stuff', or you may get bold and add on another project to your week. There are no boundaries, nothing to stop you dreaming up more and more things to do with your life. Why? Because you are master of your own destiny, of your life and how it pans out. You will always have to do the things that you can't control, but getting a better balance in your life can change your mood dramatically. As soon as you have a focus you have a purpose and with purpose comes value to your existence.

SUMMARY

What are the things you once loved to do?
What can you do to bring meaning to your life?
Start with just one project.
Does it make you forget your stress and
depression?

A Slice of Life

Financially, we live in a world where nobody truly gets rich. If you're on a low income it seems that inflation rises at a higher percentage rate than your wages do, if you get an annual wage rise at all. And if you're extremely rich and you've spent your life working really hard to get to that stage you can wave goodbye to about half of everything to the tax man! It's a question of understanding that fact and managing your life to make it work. It is possible to have money in your pocket, just don't up size your life every time your income rises. It's also worth remembering that the Beatles were singing about the tax man back in the sixties. Some things never change!

Useless Lad

I used to play the violin, I used to ride my bike
The teachers couldn't handle me, they said I
was "a tike!"
PE was done in underpants, I never had my kit
And though my tutors hated me, I couldn't give
a shit
School days were meant for others and meant
nothing to me
So exam results that I had got, a pop star I
would be
I did become a musician and made a bob or two
But "Get a proper job" they said, but what else
could I do
I was a docker for a while, by the ships, in a hut
I sat
I couldn't stand the wind and rain, I was no
good at that
I worked inside a post office, by the counter I
would sit
But the company was none too great, my
colleague would sit and knit
I've nothing against a past time, but it didn't
float my boat
And when I made a mess of things I was asked
to get my coat
I started doing voiceovers, I wasn't bad at all
But I tired of selling "Carpets, made to measure!
Shag pile wall to wall!"
I finally took up radio and haven't done so bad
And I think of the days back at my school
"Young man you're a useless lad!"

Bringing value to others

This is another lovely way to improve your mind in a positive way. I know we've talked about the fact that sometimes we try and be all things to all people, but now and then it can be a fantastic thing to do. Helping others, or giving advice on something is relatively easy. You may have a wealth of knowledge that you've just taken for granted, things that you have learnt throughout your life that you can impart to others. The older you get the more wisdom you collect. You, yes you, may be the all-seeing oracle!

There have been several times in my life where I've seen massive potential in someone. It's that person who comes along who is keen as mustard and desperate to get on in life. All they lack is the knowledge and wisdom to do that...... enter stage left... you!

Now you may not have all the answers, but you can bet your life you've got some suggestions, based on past experience. Use those past experiences to pass on some words of wisdom. Help that person by guiding them through some suggestions that might help further their career, or their life choices. It's about recycling. Don't throw away all that knowledge of how you got things to work out for you, pass it on if you've finished with it. You'll find that the people who really want to get on in life will suck it up in bucket loads. Remember though, you're not their mentor, you're just trying to add to their pot of knowledge, trying to help them make a go of things.

Helping others is such a positive thing to do and it's not about saying how clever you are, it's about giving unconditionally to someone else because you can. Inside you will feel *so* much better, that you gave something positive to someone else and what do you know, you just upped your positive well being too! You never know, in years to come they may be in a position to help and guide you and the recycling starts again!

Summary
Look out for those people who may need a little help, or guidance.
Pool your life experiences to use again.
It's about recycling.

A Slice of Life

It's easy to let people get the better of you when they impose themselves upon you. It's easy to let them do it, but it can really weigh you down. There will always be people in the world ready to tell you just how great they are. You may be just as great and probably better than them, but you find yourself listening to them banging on! You don't have to put up with people like this, they won't improve your mood, or your depressive state. Now and then it's worth standing up to them and it'll make you feel so much better.

Here's another example from my time abroad. I'd been working on another cruise ship for six weeks as a piano player and after each gig all the entertainers used to meet up in the bar. This one guy, who used to sing in the shows, would constantly go on about how great he had been that night, how the audience had loved him. He would say stupid things like..."I went on that stage tonight like a worm, but I came off feeling like a snake rearing up!" Really..... really! So after six weeks of this constant verbal nonsense I told him in no uncertain terms to (eh emm – slight cough) go away! It wasn't like me and everyone around me was surprised, but I couldn't bear the thought of another four month listening to him going on. It was a little rude and I don't advocate proceeding in this manner, but the premise is the same. Tell people if you're not happy with them and you'll probably find you get on much better, they will stop bringing you down, or at the very least wearying your brain and the world will keep turning!

Remember, people that you have to listen to talking nonsense is time you'll never get back and frankly I'd rather be off doing one of my projects whilst boosting my own confidence. Frankly, I'd rather count the hairs on my arm than listen to someone who just loves the sound of their own voice!

Giving back

Have all my days been given for nought
Every deal I've struck, every hair brain thought
The things I've learnt make me who I am
Its knowledge collected, I believe I can
Make a difference to others, the sacrificial lamb
But there's no sacrifice in giving away
What I've learnt through the years
What has come my way
There will always be someone who clamours for
more
Of the collection of thoughts I cannot ignore
I've learnt to do right when I could have done
wrong
I've travelled so far and the journey was long
And giving to others, no pay in return
Is payment enough if others will learn
We don't always realise there's so much to give
But our lives have been fruitful, the way we
have lived
So have all my days been given for nought?
No, the experiences captured are by someone
else caught

<u>Having a slight wobble</u>

If you get up and running and find that your life is gradually starting to feel better that's great, but as I said earlier, watch out for signs that it's about to keel over. I've had several "wobbles" and it can take a while to get back to where you were before. It doesn't mean you've failed. Anything you have done in however small a way is success, but depression will always try and get the better of you. Don't let it! All the work you have done has not been wasted, it just needs resetting. Just like a computer, now and then you need to re-boot. If you're really struggling it's definitely worth going back to your doctor, or getting a bit more counselling. I bet if you tell them what you've achieved so far they will be amazed and will support you one hundred percent.

So let's think about the plus and minus again. Take a look at what you'd achieved before your wobble. Scribble them down on the back pages. Start introducing all the positives back into your daily life. You see, you weren't doing too bad after all! Now take a look at all the things that didn't go to plan. Write each one down and then go through them one at a time. What was it you were trying to achieve? Why didn't they work out? What can you do to get them up and running and part of your life? Just by figuring out the positives and negatives you're already back on track, doing something to improve your depression.

Summary

Look out for that wobble.

Start again – reboot!

Get more professional advice if that will help.

Start listing the positives and negatives.

Plan a new way forward.

A Slice of Life

There will always be people who want to waste your time, because they enjoy being around others. Sometimes you just want to go it alone and not be given advice on the best way to do this or that. Also, be conscious that this isn't the behaviour you show to other. When my wife and I got together there were numerous times when our parents tried to give us advice. "You want to do it this way, or that way." It's always well-meaning so try not to take it the wrong way. I'm sure we do this to our daughter, but personally I try and give her the options as I know them and then it's up to her to make her own choices. She's a grown up, not twelve any more.

Anyway, whilst she *was* twelve we had a caravan. We had years of great holiday fun and I'll never forget those times. However, there were always people on the caravan sites who wanted to come knocking at your door.

"Hello. I see you've got the six five hundred double glazed windows on your van. Tricky if you ever get a dead fly stuck in between. I know how to fix that!"

They chuckle and you stare in amazement. You see the odd fly had never been a problem on our holidays. We never stayed awake at night wondered what ever we could do. We slept peacefully and excited about our next day's adventure.

"So, you've got the Aqua B twenty eight taps in your kitchen. Great whilst they work but eventually the pump will go and you'll need the

C thirty eight replacement if you want it to last any amount of time. I've found that a complete re wire will help."

At this point you want to shout, "GO AWAY." These people are watching you, waiting for their moment to pounce. Like an aggressive animal, never make eye contact with them. Enjoy your break and keep away from them. They are the people who never leave the site, it's all about the caravan and not the new places they could be exploring. (And yes, it's true, they do more often than not wear pale coloured jumpers with yellow diamonds on the front.)

You will find these people in all walks of life, for us they were prevalent during our caravanning years. We always considered ourselves to be a family that went away in a caravan.... not Caravaners.

A place of sanctuary

There will be plenty of time when you just can't get your head straight. If you can, try and get away for an hour. Maybe take this book with you. Make some more notes. Finding a place can be tricky if you live in a big community with people everywhere. I'm very lucky to live in a place that has the Lake District on one side of me and the Pennines on the other. As beautiful as The Lakes are it's usually full of visitors, unless it's the dead of winter. However, if I drive for fifteen minutes I can be up on the Pennines looking down across the fells and the Eden valley. This is where I come to think, to be alone, with only the sheep to bother me. If there isn't a quiet place that you can go to there are other options.

Many years ago, for four hours a month, I rented a room above a shop. It allowed me peace and quiet to think and to do some writing for an hour a week. It brought massive value to me at that time and began a new chapter in my life which continues today. Here I am still writing, still publishing books. Perhaps you know someone who can let you use their shed, or caravan on a quiet bit of land.

Interestingly, the first book I wrote and published was all done whilst suffering with depression. It proves that you can still continue to live your life and do things if you manage it in the right way.

So I say a big thank you to the Pennines as this is where I've sat, in my car, radio on quietly in the background, writing this book. It's a bit rainy and blustery today and the view of the fells comes and goes with a blanket of mist moving south west to north east. Every now and then there's a break in the cloud cover where the sun shines through, down onto distant farms and villages. Occassionally I stop typing to sit on my cold hands, so it's probably time to call it a day and head home.

Summary
Find a place to go where you can be on your own
Use the time to focus on your thoughts without interruption
Also, allow your mind the freedom to wander a bit.
(It's probably formulating new plans)
Take the book and a pen with you
(And maybe a flask of hot coffee)

A Slice of Life

News on TV, radio and online can be really depressing. How many times have you heard reports on a story starting like this... "There's been a major accident on the motorway involving five cars and a lorry. Police were called to the scene and two lanes were closed whilst the incident was dealt with." And then when all the harrowing details are listed we discover that apart from one person being taken to hospital with a broken arm there were no other injuries and no fatalities. So why could we not be told the good bit of the news first? Well because it's doesn't provide the same sensational effect if you tell it that way round. It might be worth being a little more analytical when absorbing breaking news.

We also hear so much political rhetoric and stock phrases. "Today we are sending a message to our enemies." How about communicating with them, call them up, send them an email and God forbid, get around the table and talk things out. Of course politician's use certain phrases and babble speak because if they don't the press have a field day with them. Watch out for any public speaker who dares to wear their heart on their sleeve, they are very quickly stamped upon. So they continue to talk about the 'working family', the 'man on the street' and will often start their sentence with the word 'look' to somehow provide some authority to what it is they're saying, a show that they're being frank and honey with you. (Call me an old cynic!)

Now I'm not saying that because the way our news is served up we should ignore it, most of us want to know what's going on in the world, but we are in control of how we digest it these days. Get a news app on your phone or tablet. Change the newspaper you read and even then only read selected pages. You can decide what news you want and how you get it. I have an app on my tablet that will every now and then flash up a breaking story, so I just get the headline. If I want to know more I can delve in and look more closely at certain stories. We don't have to wait for the news on the telly anymore. We can get our news whenever we want it and to the degree that we want it too. Let's have a bit of a laugh at politicians and the way they speak. Most of them work really hard and have just fallen into the trap of taking on a public speaking persona. *Look*, I'm sure that when they're not talking about the 'working man', they're at home laughing about themselves.

A place of Sanctuary

Silence, save for the wind is mine
My mind is still, this place to dine
It feeds my soul to have such peace
No vile taste will my mind release
Dramatic view, this surely must
Be canvas daubed with green and rust
Could any scene be so profound?
Or by a Constable be yet found
To capture what is in my view
No painter, dead or alive, could do.
The rolling fells are mine alone
A finer sight I've never known.
Blencathra and to Saddleback
Reminding me I never lack
The joy and splendour brought to me
Goddess of nature sets me free
And as I ponder this scene of might
I remember Wordsworth ....and Wainright

Finale

Well it's time for you to take a bow. The applause is all for you! Just by reading my book you've achieved so much by giving yourself plenty to think about. I don't have all the answers, but there's a chance I may have acted, in some small way, as the catalyst that has reset your mind so that you can find the answers for yourself. There's always going to be so much to do before the next performance (and let's be honest you won't always remember all your lines.) However, I hope you feel more empowered and stronger to take on every new day in the best way you can.

We live in a crazy world that will continually try and throw you off track..... DON'T LET IT! Always look at the plus and minus effect, take small steps to change who you are, to become who you want to be and one day you will run faster than you ever thought possible.

Run wild and free...... sunrise for the simple!

NOTES

NOTES

NOTES

NOTES

NOTES

NOTES

NOTES